Preparing Better Teacher-Made Tests: A Practical Guide

by
Frank J. Sparzo

Library of Congress Catalog Card Number 90-62018
ISBN 0-87367-311-5
Copyright © 1990 by the Phi Delta Kappa Educational Foundation
Bloomington, Indiana

This fastback is sponsored by the Central Michigan University Chapter of Phi Delta Kappa, which made a generous contribution toward publication costs.

Table of Contents

Introduction

One of the old adages in education is that the single best way to evaluate teachers is to inspect the tests they give their students. Good teaching and good testing go hand in hand. That is so because well-constructed tests constitute a very important means by which teachers motivate and direct student learning, determine how well students are achieving instructional objectives, and assess how well they are teaching.

There are many reasons why teacher-made tests may be inadequate. While teachers may have had experience constructing a few test items as part of a course in tests and measurement, few have been asked to develop a complete test (using a test blueprint), give the test to students, and change it in accordance with an analysis of student responses. Moreover, some teachers put off test construction to the last minute; constructing a test in haste and without reference to instructional objectives will surely fail to motivate and direct student learning.

There are many other common mistakes made by teachers when constructing tests. Some ask too many low-level questions. Others rely on test items supplied by a textbook publisher, unaware that these items may not be good or appropriate (content valid) items for what is going on in their classroom.

Many teacher-made test questions are of poor quality because they are technically inadequate. For example, if an item has two or more correct answers that depend on different but legitimate interpretations of the item, then the test suffers from item ambiguity.

In the case of true-false tests, a distinct tendency to ask more true than false questions will provide an unintended clue to correct answers. Also, there is evidence that false items discriminate among high and low achieving students somewhat better than true items. Thus a teacher might be better off asking more false than true questions.

Finally, many teachers at all levels of education do not analyze student responses to test items in order to check on the quality of their tests. There are several relatively simple analytic techniques available that can help teachers improve their tests. For example, simply counting the responses that high-achieving and low-achieving students make to each objective item on a test can reveal how well an item discriminates between these two groups as well as suggest what might be done to improve the item.

Although the foregoing problems are far from rare, the good news is that much is known about constructing effective classroom tests. Any teacher can use this knowledge to improve his or her skills in measurement and evaluation.

This fastback is about writing good test items, a task faced by most teachers at all levels of education. Although my main concern is with the construction of test items, mere technical facility in writing items is of little value if they do not clearly reflect the objectives of instruction. I am assuming that teachers are thoroughly familiar with course content and are skilled in written expression. Nothing said about test construction will substitute for competent teaching. Thus this fastback is designed to help good teachers write better items than they might otherwise write.

This introductory chapter touches on some of the problems associated with preparing classroom tests. The second chapter outlines five steps in preparing a test, the PLAN-WRITE System. The third chapter describes the do's and don'ts of writing commonly used test items. The last chapter will provide practice in applying these suggestions.

This fastback concentrates on but one aspect of the complex process of measurement and evaluation: writing technically correct test items that are compatible with your instructional objectives. You must decide how far you want to extend your knowledge and skills beyond the rudiments presented in these pages. Should you decide to continue, the resources at the end of this fastback should be of help. But whatever you decide, you will find many useful suggestions that can lead to writing better test items.

Preparing Teacher-Made Tests

You can prepare good classroom tests by following five basic steps. We shall refer to these steps as the PLAN-WRITE System. The steps are:

1. Prepare a content outline.
2. List instructional objectives.
3. Appraise student performance levels.
4. Note content, objectives, and levels in a test blueprint.
5. Write test items.

Ideally, the PLAN-WRITE system should be implemented *before* instruction; doing so can help you plan instruction. And if you share the test blueprint (Step 4) with your students, as some specialists recommend, you can help them prepare for your tests.

Let us now examine each step in turn.

Step One: Prepare Content Outline

Review your notes, assignments, and textbook materials; then outline the areas of content that your test items will cover. For example, for a unit on American government, a partial outline might look like this:

Content Outline

Content	Emphasis
Vocabulary	20%
Federalism	
Popular Sovereignty	
Pocket Veto	
Judicial Review	
Facts/Principles	60%
Three branches of government	
How a bill becomes a law	
Special powers of the House	
Amending the Constitution	
Applications	20%
Interviewing government officials	
Reporting on a town meeting	

Although categories will differ, it is important to note two things about good content outlines. First, content should closely match what you do and what you require your students to do during instruction. It is neither fair nor good practice to base test items on material that has been ignored or neglected during instruction. This is a content validity issue. Second, you will need to estimate in percentage terms the amount of emphasis each part of the outline received during instruction. This percentage appears in the right column of the outline. These estimates will be the basis for determining what proportion of your test will be devoted to each part of the outline. For example, assuming that 50 items have been prepared, about 10 items should be concerned with vocabulary (20% of 50), 30 should cover facts/principles, and 10 should measure student learning in the area of applications.

Step Two: List Instructional Objectives

Good test preparation requires good instructional objectives, which can be assessed in terms of observable behavior or performance. A behavior or performance objective is a statement about what students will be able to do or perform after instruction. Behavioral objectives identify behavior, outcomes, or products that are directly observable. For example, we can directly observe a person playing the violin, talking, writing, and so on. Similarly, we can directly observe outcomes or products: a misspelled word, a complete or incomplete worksheet, a science project, an essay. Good behavioral statements make use of action verbs, such as listing, pronouncing, reciting, selecting, and solving.

Good instructional objectives serve three main functions: 1) they help teachers focus on important learning experiences, 2) they communicate expectations to students and others, and 3) they suggest ways to evaluate learning. As a demonstration of the usefulness of behavioral objectives in preparing a test, consider the following objectives.

Objective 1: To understand the differences among the three branches of government.

Objective 2: To identify correct and incorrect examples of executive, legislative, and judicial action.

Objective 2 more clearly defines your task (you need to provide examples); it lets your students know what you expect (they will have to choose from among examples); and it suggests the kind of test items you might write (perhaps multiple-choice items, which present new examples).

When writing instructional objectives, avoid words and phrases like appreciates, comprehends, knows, learns, understands, reads with ease, etc. These and many other words and phrases do not refer to directly observable behavior. We cannot see "thinking," "understanding," or a student's "interest." The existence or nonexistence of these things can only be inferred from observable performance or products.

Good behavioral objectives must include a standard or criterion of performance in addition to the specification of directly observable behavior. Many writers also recommend a third component: the conditions under which performance occurs. An example of an acceptable objective would be, "Students will point out the puns in three unfamiliar passages with at least 90% accuracy."

Stating good instructional or performance objectives can serve important teaching, learning, and evaluative functions, as we have seen. But there is no guarantee that they will do so. Writing technically correct instructional objectives is one thing; writing important or worthwhile ones is another.

Fortunately, there are several things teachers can do to guard against writing educationally unimportant objectives. That is the subject of the third step in PLAN-WRITE.

Step Three: Appraise Performance Levels

The third step in preparing a test is inseparable from Step 2. As you list your instructional objectives, you must include objectives that call for different levels of cognition or thinking. Benjamin Bloom and his colleagues have developed a taxonomy of instructional objectives that uses a hierarchy or levels of thinking. The six levels can serve as a basis for developing test items that assess different types of instructional objectives. The six levels are:

- Knowledge
- Comprehension
- Application
- Analysis
- Synthesis
- Evaluation

Knowledge is the simplest level of cognitive performance and evaluation is the highest and most complex. The basic idea behind the hierarchy is that higher-level performances include and are dependent on lower-level ones. We may think of the first four levels (knowledge, comprehension, application, analysis) as relating generally to understanding concepts and principles, while the last two (synthesis and evaluation) relate to more creative endeavors. The following discussion on each of the six levels will clarify their relevance to instructional objectives and test item construction.

Knowledge. An objective written at this level requires students to reproduce something in more or less the same form as it was presented, for example, asking students to produce a list of memorized words, to repeat the solution to a specific problem, or to state facts verbatim. Action verbs used in objectives written at this level include define, identify, label, name, recall, recite, recognize, select, and state. Knowledge-level objectives are relatively easy to write and are very prevalent in education; in fact, they usually overshadow higher-level objectives.

Comprehension. At this level, students must not merely reproduce something, they must understand it to the point of changing it in some way. For example, when you ask your students to summarize or paraphrase what they have heard or read, to give their own example of something, to translate from one language to another, or to read music, you are calling for responses at the comprehension level. Action verbs associated with this level include explain, convert, generalize, interpret, and predict.

Application. Objectives that require students to use a principle, rule, generalization, or strategy in an unfamiliar setting qualify as application objectives. These objectives go beyond comprehension in that they require students to use ideas, principles, and theories, not merely to paraphrase or explain them. If, for example, you asked students to collect and classify insects found in their neighborhoods after teaching the principles of classification, you would be calling for behavior at the application level. If the students collect and classify only those insects already studied in class, their performance represents comprehension, not application. Action verbs associated with application objectives include choose, compute, demonstrate, employ, implement, produce, relate, and solve.

Analysis. An analysis objective calls for students to break down something unfamiliar into its basic parts. It also may require a focus on the relations among the parts. Analysis depends on skills from lower performance levels: knowledge (knowing what to look for), comprehension (translating a concept or principle), and application (relating translated knowledge to the problem at hand). Words and phrases associated with this level include deduce cause and effect, diagram, distinguish, infer mood or purpose, note unstated assumptions, outline, select relevant particulars, and subdivide.

Synthesis. Objectives written at this level require students to produce something original or unique. Unlike previous levels, there usually is no one best or right answer (although judgments are made about the quality of performance). Synthesis objectives call on students to respond to unfamiliar problems by putting things together or combining elements in original ways. When you ask your students to write an original essay, poem, story, or musical composition, you are calling on them to be creative. You also are helping them become mature learners. Words associated with synthesis objectives include categorize, devise, discover, formulate, and invent.

Evaluation. At this level students are required to judge the quality or value of an idea, method, product, or human performance that has a specified purpose and to include reasons for their judgment. Asking students to judge the quality of a play, to make up titles for a play, or to create a new play and to provide a rationale for their responses represents performance at this level. As in the case of synthesis, there is usually no one best or correct answer. Thus objective test items may fail to adequately measure complex objectives written at the levels of synthesis and evaluation. Verbs commonly associated with this category include appraise, assess, compare, criticize, and justify.

After preparing a content outline, listing instructional objectives, and appraising levels of performance, you are ready to combine all three in a test blueprint. That is the fourth step in PLAN-WRITE.

Step Four: The Test Blueprint

Test blueprints can help teachers avoid the test preparation problems mentioned earlier. Of course, describing steps in the preparation of a test is much easier than applying them. Outlining course content and writing objectives that reflect different levels of performance is hard work. But the payoff is a content-valid test that requires students to think at all cognitive levels.

An example of a test blueprint is shown in Figure 1. It is sketchy, but it does illustrate the basic features of good test construction. Listed to the left are a few illustrative objectives that reflect course content. To the right are the six performance levels. The numbers tell us two things: how many items will be written for each objective and the performance level of the items. Thus, in the case of the first objective listed, the teacher will write eight items to test student vocabulary, four of these will test at the knowledge level and four at the level of comprehension. Item percentages reflect the teacher's estimate of the emphasis received by each major part of the content outline. Finally, as you can see, the test will have a total of 50 items.

When you have built a good test blueprint, you are well on your way to preparing a content-valid test. And that takes us to the last step in PLAN-WRITE.

Step Five: Write Test Items

The rest of this fastback is devoted to writing good test items. Although teachers use a variety of ways to observe student behavior (work samples, checklists, rating scales, self-report devices), we shall focus on test items, especially those that teachers use most often — true-false, multiple-choice, matching, completion, and essay items.

| | Performance Levels | | | | | | | |
| | Number of Items | | | | | | | |
	Knowledge	Comprehension	Application	Analysis	Synthesis	Evaluation	Total	Percent
Vocabulary								
1. Students will define velocity, speed - - -	4	4					8	16%
2. - - -	1	1					2	4%
Facts/Principles								
1. Working from a list of animals and environments, students will match animals and habitats.	3						3	6%
2. Students will calculate force for objects of different mass and acceleration.			1				1	2%
3. Students will decide whether statements are consistent with Darwinian views.			6				6	12%
4. When given unfamiliar diagrams, students will answer questions about the genetic processes involved.		2					2	4%
5. - - -	2						2	4%
6. - - -	1	9	3	2	1		16	32%
Applications								
1. In response to an unfamiliar passage, students will infer author's assumptions about the role of science in everyday life.				5			5	10%
2. Students will critique an unfamiliar experiment.						5	5	10%
Total	11	16	10	7	1	5	50	

The first four (true-false, multiple-choice, matching, and completion) are considered objective items, in that those who score them end up with the same score (barring clerical errors). Essays are considered subjective items in that those who score them often end up with different scores. Sometimes true-false, multiple-choice, and matching items are referred to as fixed-response items (students must choose from the options offered), while completion and essay items are referred to as free-response or supply-type items (students supply their own answers). Since too much freedom of response may lead to variability in scoring, care must be taken in writing completion items.

It is important to point out that test construction is more art than science. This is especially true of teacher-made tests. Thus many of the suggestions for preparing a test are more a matter of expert judgment than of scientific verification. There is some evidence that well-prepared teacher-made tests are as reliable (consistent in measurement) as many standardized tests and even more valid for a particular student or class.

The next chapter will provide some do's and don'ts for writing commonly used types of test items.

Writing Test Items

This section begins with some general guidelines that apply to writing test items. Later, suggestions specific to each type of item will be offered. No guideline is correct for all situations, so use a little common sense if a guideline seems inappropriate.

1. *Make certain that the performance called for in your test item closely matches that specified in your objective.* This is the most important guideline of them all. For example, one of the objectives from the test blueprint presented in Figure 1 was, "Students will calculate force for objects of different mass and acceleration." A multiple-choice test item asking, "Which of the following formulas is used to determine force?" clearly would not meet that objective.

2. *Eliminate trivia.* Each test item should measure an important aspect of the subject matter. Deciding whether an item is trivial requires a judgment call. Answering these questions might help make this judgment: Does the item test something worth knowing? Will responding correctly make a difference in the competency level of my students? If you answer "no" or "maybe not," you have probably written an unimportant item.

3. *Stay away from textbook language.* A slavish reliance on the text will almost certainly lead to low-level items.

4. *Strive to write objectives and test items that call for higher-level performances.* This guideline is a corollary to the previous one. Compare the items below. Both deal with the interference effects of our actions on memory; but only one follows the guideline.

1) Forgetting something you learned yesterday because you learned something else today is an instance of:
   a. interference
   b. proaction
   c. decoding
   d. disassociation

2) If you wanted to make practical use of the research on forgetting, what would you recommend to a friend who has but two hours to prepare for next week's 8:00 a.m. exam?
   a. Study a week in advance
   b. Prepare the night before
   c. Study two consecutive hours
   d. Prepare at least one day before

The first question is probably measuring only memory. The second is at least an application item, if we assume that the problem is a new one for the student. With a little thought, many lower-level items can be converted to higher-level ones. Incidentally, the ability to formulate higher-level items is indicative of one's command of the subject matter.

5. *Write unambiguous questions.* Your questions must have unmistakable meanings and not be open to more than one equally reasonable interpretation. Note the ambiguity in the following item.

1) Governments are very dissimilar in the way they operate. (True or False)

Unless the teacher or text actually made the statement, the item is unanswerable because it is ambiguous. Who is to say what "very dissimilar" and "in the way they operate" mean? And if the teacher or text did make the statement, the item is a good candidate for a trivia award.

6. *Make certain that objective items have answers that are clearly correct — answers that experts could accept.* Asking colleagues to respond to your items can help. Asking competent students for feedback also can help.

7. *Arrange items in an order that differs from that used during instruction.* If this is not done, students may profit from "order clues" when answering questions. A useful technique is to begin your test with a few relatively easy items. Then choose items in random order so they do not follow the sequence of the text or your presentations.

8. *Watch for items that cue answers to other items.* Do you recall getting this kind of help on exams?

9. *Make items independent of one another.* An answer to one item should not depend on knowing the answer to some other item.

10. *Keep the reading level simple.* Constructing items using technical words that are related to the subject being tested is acceptable practice; making the reading level of items difficult by using unfamiliar or uncommon words is not (unless, of course, one's goal is to assess vocabulary or reading skill).

11. *Indicate the source of an opinion.* It is unfair to ask students to endorse something that is largely a matter of opinion. The second true-false item below is better than the first because it follows this guideline.

1) Martin Luther King acted on the basis of postconventional moral principles. (True or False)

2) According to the authors, Martin Luther King acted on the basis of postconventional moral principles. (True or False)

12. *Try preparing your questions long before using them.* Following this suggestion will promote thoughtful questions. An added bonus is having time to review and revise items in need of repair.

So much for general guidelines. We now turn to specific guidelines for writing objective and essay questions. At times, one or more of the above guidelines may be repeated as they relate to specific types of items.

True-False Test Items

True-false items have been criticized by both lay and professional people. It is said, for example, that true-false tests are ambiguous, measure trivia, promote rote learning, and are prone to error because they encourage guessing. And, of course, poorly written true-false items suffer from all of these problems. But there is not much research evidence that these are inherent problems. Consider, for example, the following items. Assuming that the questions posed are new to the student, are they ambiguous? Trivial? Do they measure rote learning?

1. A man firmly believes that murder is a crime because it is wrong. This belief illustrates stage 4 in moral development.
2. If a perfect inverse relationship existed between complaining and having friends, the more one complained the fewer friends one would have.

The first item was designed to test student understanding of Lawrence Kohlberg's moral stages of development. The second is concerned with the interpretation of the correlation coefficient. The point is that true-false items skillfully written can be unambiguous, call for worthwhile learning, and need not measure only rote learning.

Blind guessing is a potential problem with true-false items. But since there is some evidence that few students resort to blind guessing ("informed guessing" is more likely), the problem may have been exaggerated. To combat the problem of guessing, students are sometimes asked to correct false statements by indicating why they are false. In such cases the scoring of the items may no longer remain objective. Using formulas to "correct" for guessing on teacher-made tests is not recommended by testing experts, unless many students do not have time to complete tests.

True-false items are sometimes thought to be easy to prepare; but this advantage is more apparent than real. It takes hard work and skill to write good items. But if good items are written, two advantages follow: 1) they provide a simple and direct way to measure student achievement, and 2) they are efficient — they provide many independent, scorable responses per unit of test time. True-false items can sample much of what a student has learned and are especially useful when asking questions about stimulus materials such as films, maps, diagrams, and graphs.

True-False Item Guidelines

1. Base the item on a single idea or proposition. Single-idea questions are relatively easy to understand. They are also more likely to be better questions than those that are longer and more complex. Thus item A below is acceptable; but item B, because it expresses two ideas, is not.

A) Measurement and evaluation are synonymous terms.
B) Measurement refers to assigning numbers systematically, while evaluation refers to making judgments about the meaning of assigned numbers.

2. Write items that test an important point.

3 Avoid lifting statements directly from the class text. Some teachers, for example, merely insert "not" in a statement taken from the text. Unless memorizing exact content is essential, this approach will seldom lead to good results.

4. Be concise. Your questions should be as brief as possible.

5. Write clearly true or clearly false items. It is not necessary to write perfectly true or perfectly false items so long as the answers are defensible — that is, so long as well-informed people would agree with keyed answers. Writing items in pairs can help you do this. One item should be true, the other false. You will, of course, choose only one item from a pair for the test.

6. Eliminate giveaways. Giveaways are unintended clues to correct answers. Let us take a look at three of these.

a) True statements tend to be longer than false ones, due perhaps to the addition of qualifying words to make an item true. Item length may then cue correct answers. Make your true and false items approximately equal in length.

b) Some teachers have a tendency to write many more true than false questions or many more false than true questions. When students catch on to this, they benefit from a second kind of giveaway. Thus approximately half your items should be true and half false. However, because there is evidence that false statements discriminate between high and low achieving students better than true ones do (people tend to answer "true" when in doubt), you may want to include a few more false items.

c) The use of specific determiners (extreme words and certain modifiers) can cause trouble. Because completely true statements are rare, strongly worded statements are likely to be false. Thus try to avoid such words as all, always, never, only, nothing, and alone. Many students know that these words are likely to be found in false statements. Words or phrases like may, could, as a rule, sometimes, often, in general, occasionally, and usually should be avoided also because they are associated with true items. If you must on occasion use a specific determiner, use it in a way contrary to expectation.

Some readers at this point may think that these guidelines and those that follow are designed to trap or trick students. This is not the case. A test that allowed a student to get 5 of 25 questions right because of item length or specific determiners would not be measuring knowledge. The more one allows this kind of student response, the less valid one's test is likely to be.

7. Beware of words denoting indefinite degree. The use of words like more, less, important, unimportant, large, small, recent, old, tall, great, and so on, can easily lead to ambiguity.

8. State items positively. Negative statements may be difficult to interpret. This is especially true of statements using a double nega-

tive (which should not be used in any type of test item). In addition, even well-prepared students can easily overlook such words as not or never. If on rare occasions a negative word is used, be sure to underline or capitalize it.

9. Beware of detectable answer patterns. Test-wise students can detect answer patterns (TTTFFFF) designed to make scoring easier.

Multiple-Choice Test Items

Test specialists regard the multiple-choice item highly, thus their widespread use on standardized achievement and aptitude tests. However, critics of multiple-choice items complain about poorly written items.

One of the critics' complaints is that multiple-choice questions measure little more than vocabulary, isolated facts, and trivia; and very often they are right. But in skilled hands, multiple-choice items can be impressively adaptable in measuring many important educational outcomes.

The basic components of multiple-choice questions are the item stem, which presents a problem, and several response options (usually 3 to 5), which follow under the stem. One of the options is correct or clearly the best answer to the problem. The other options (distractors) are designed to be attractive to the uninformed.

The "interpretive exercise" format is widely used in standardized testing because it provides a potentially excellent means to test higher levels of achievement or aptitude. This format presents the testee with a paragraph, graph, picture, poetry, work of art, musical composition, or any other complex material. The student is then asked a series of questions that require interpretation, application, analysis, synthesis, or evaluative thinking. If you have not done so, try your hand at using this format. It is capable of tapping many forms of high level performance.

Multiple-Choice Item Guidelines

1. Select the format of the item with care. Although there are several variations of the multiple-choice format, those that follow can serve you well.

   a) To make reading easy, response options are listed vertically rather than arranged in tandem.
   b) Response options follow logically and grammatically from the item stem.
   c) The stem presents a complete problem (more about this later).
   d) No punctuation marks are used when options contain numbers (they might be misread as decimals).
   e) All items need not have the same number of response options.

2. State a clearly formulated problem in the stem. The examinee should not have to complete the problem by consulting the response options. The stem may be either a complete question or an incomplete sentence, so long as a specific problem is formulated. It is probably a good idea to formulate a complete question whenever you can. Consider this item:

Mars is
   a. closer to the sun than Jupiter
   b. 93,000,000 miles from the sun
   c. the third closest planet to the sun

Because the stem fails to present a complete problem, the item is functioning as a true-false item. Its stem is much like these item stems: "Which of the following is true?" and "Select the false statement from the following." "Multiple-choice" questions of this sort should probably be cast in a true-false format.

3. State item stems positively. Negatively stated stems not only may lead to confusion, they may fail to reflect the kinds of problems students experience in everyday life.

26

If on rare occasions a negative word is used (not, never), be sure to underline or capitalize it. The advice with respect to double negatives — a negative in the stem and in one or more of the response options — is even stronger: Eliminate them entirely.

4. Write the stem so that the answer is placed at the end. Thus the first stem below is preferable to the second.

a) The term for the chemical activities of all living things is _____.

b) _____ refers to the chemical activities of all living things.

5. Be creative. This guideline challenges you to take advantage of the versatility of the multiple-choice item for measuring important educational outcomes. Strive for this arbitrary goal: At least half of the items will be above the knowledge level.

6. Be concise. Being concise not only promotes clarity of expression, but saves valuable testing time as well.

7. Make all distractors plausible. There should be a degree of truth in each distractor in order for the uninformed to find them attractive. If it is unlikely that anyone would choose an option, why include it at all? On occasion, even two options would be preferable to offering implausible distractors.

8. Make certain there is only one clearly best answer.

9. Avoid using the options "all of these" and "none of these." These options tend to be overused by those who have difficulty formulating plausible distractors. They also are associated with item ambiguity. Neither should be used unless the answer to an item is absolutely correct.

10. Eliminate unnecessary repetition. If a phrase is repeated in each response item, add it to the stem. This eliminates unnecessary words. The more students engage in unnecessary reading, the fewer questions they can respond to per unit of test time.

11. Eliminate giveaways. Let us consider five kinds of giveaways in multiple-choice items.

a) Test-wise students can detect any tendency to make correct answers longer than distractors. The remedy is to make your response options approximately equal in length.
b) Test-wise students also can spot specific determiners when they are used in item stems and response options. Watch for them.
c) Using the same or similar words in both the item stem and the correct answer can give away the answer.
d) Beware of grammatical giveaways. For example, if the stem ends with the word "an" and only one or two options begin with a vowel, then the student can easily eliminate distractors. Similarly, if the stem has a singular verb and one or more of the options are plural, students are given an extra clue to the correct answer.
e) Alert students may detect any tendency to prefer certain response options. For example, students may learn that option "c" is most often correct or that option "a" is seldom correct.

12. Order response options. Arrange response options in some logical sequence, if possible. This will help students locate choices. Names could be ordered alphabetically, dates chronologically, formulas in terms of complexity, and so on.

Matching-Test Items

A matching-test item format typically consists of two columns: a premise set on the left and a response set on the right. Students are asked to match items in the two columns. Further, there are a variety of matching formats that differ in complexity from the simple two-column format. For example, matching items can call for students to select an author and a concept for each descriptive statement listed. Some of these formats can be quite demanding, requiring performances well above the memory level.

Matching items are especially effective in prompting students to see relationships among a set of items and to integrate knowledge.

However, they are less suited than multiple-choice items for measuring higher levels of performance.

Matching-Test Item Guidelines

1. Provide directions. Students should not have to ask, for example, whether options may be used more than once.

2. Use only homogeneous material. Each item in a set should be the same kind as the other items, for example, all authors or all cities. When different kinds of items are used in each set, the associations tend to be obvious.

3. Place longer material in the left column. This will help students locate matches.

4. Arrange column material in some systematic order. For example, names can be arranged alphabetically, and so on.

5. Keep columns short. As a rule of thumb, the premise set should contain no more than 3 to 7 items; the response set should contain 2 items more than the premise set.

6. Keep an item on one page. Arrange items so that students will not have to turn pages back and forth as they respond. Placing one item on two pages can become quite frustrating to students.

Completion-Test Items

Completion items ask students to supply an *important* word, number, or phrase to complete a statement. Blanks are provided to be filled in by the student.

Completion items are especially useful in the early elementary grades where vocabulary is growing in basic subjects. They also are especially effective in mathematics and science when answers to problems require computation. Completion items are easy to write and provide efficient measurement. And they are not as susceptible to guessing as are true-false and multiple-choice items.

But there are drawbacks. Questions can easily be turned into subjective items, in which responses would vary so greatly that subjectivity would enter into scoring. Another drawback is that completion items are more suited to measuring lower-level than higher-level performances, except when problems are presented, as in the case of mathematics and science.

Completion-Test Item Guidelines

1. Call for answers that can be scored objectively. Prefer single words and short phrases. Check your items by posing this critical question: Can someone with no competency in the subject score the items objectively by relying solely on the answer key?

2. Prepare a scoring key that contains all acceptable answers for each item.

3. Beware of open questions. Open questions are those that invite unexpected but reasonable answers, as in the following case.

The author of *Profiles in Courage* was (<u>John F. Kennedy</u>).

But what is one to do with these answers: "President," "assassinated," "privileged"? The remedy is to close the item so there is but one answer to be scored objectively. For example, ask for "the name of the author."

Remember to key all acceptable answers. Thus a key for this item might contain John F. Kennedy, John Kennedy, J.F. Kennedy, and J. Kennedy. Some teachers might not accept just Kennedy.

4. Place blanks near the end of the statement. Try to present a complete or nearly complete statement before calling for a response.

5. Eliminate giveaways. Two giveaways are:

a) The length of the lines to the right of an item can provide clues to the correct answer. The remedy is to make all blanks of equal length.

b) Grammatical structure also can provide clues. For example, using the word "an" can alert the student to the fact that the answer begins with a vowel.

6. Limit the number of blanks to one or two per item, if possible. Statements with too many blanks waste valuable time as students attempt to figure out what is being asked.

7. If a numerical answer is called for, indicate the units in which it is to be expressed.

Items that call for more than a word or phrase are sometimes classified as restricted-essay items. It may be preferable to call them written-response items. The term "essay" can be reserved for items sharing the characteristics identified in the next section, to which we now turn.

Essay Questions

Essay items ask students to supply written answers to questions (sometimes questions and answers are oral). Judgments are then made about the accuracy and quality of their answers. Though the lines of demarcation are not clear, it is convenient to place items requiring written responses in one of three classes:

1. Written-response items These items call for answers that fall in the knowledge or comprehension categories of performance. Responses to written-response items may consist of a fact or opinion or as much as a student can remember about a specified topic. Thus answers may range in length from a sentence or two to many pages. Written-response items are very common in education. Although they can and do serve important teaching, learning, and evaluative functions, they are sometimes perjoratively referred to as "regurgitation items." Here is an example of a written-response item:

What three functions do instructional objectives serve?

2. Restricted-response essays. We shall here reserve the term essay for questions that present an unfamiliar problem to the student.

The student, in turn, recalls relevant concepts, facts, and principles; organizes these recollections; and writes a coherent and creative response to the problem. Restricted-response essays call for responses that are roughly a page or less in length. They may be distinguished from written-response items in that answers fall above the knowledge-comprehension levels of performance. Here is an example of a restricted-response essay (assume that the problem is unfamiliar to the students):

Compare verbal and nonverbal art. How are they similar? Different?

3. Extended-response essays. These differ from restricted-response essays in that the questions posed are more complex; hence they require extended answers. Extended-response essays call on a range of talents, from knowledge to evaluation. A competent evaluation of the answers also requires talent! Here is an example of an extended-response essay:

Imagine that you visit Earth in 2500 A.D. You find astonishing changes in education. Students spend more time in school, study more things, and almost never drop out. Educators no longer talk about individualizing instruction — they practice it completely. Every student is presented with different learning materials and activities. In fact, students are similar academically in only one way: Each is developing knowledge and skills in reading, writing, speaking, languages, mathematics, scientific method, problem solving, technology, and creativity. You observe that students are not given tests as you knew them, yet they are learning several times more in half the time needed in 2000 A.D. They spend half their time in artistic, literary, musical, physical, and community activities. Highly paid teachers work in teams. No one lectures. Some focus on analyzing knowledge sets; others work on instructional programming that hardly resembles that which you knew; still others provide counseling for individual students. Centuries of use have taught teachers that technology is the only means to deliver instruction fairly and effectively. You conclude that education in 2500 A.D. is characterized by three things: a highly sophisticated concern with *what* is presented to a student, a delivery system that allows complete student involvement, and a technology that provides immediate feedback for student action.

Write a well-organized essay of 400 to 600 words discussing changes in learning theory, in views toward students, and in the politics of education that might account for the educational system of 2500 A.D. You will be judged not only by what you say, but how effectively you use references. Devote approximately 30 minutes to planning, 80 to writing, and 10 for proofreading and revision.

Many educators are quite generous in their praise of essay items. It has long been said that essays provide the best overall means of assessing achievement. But this claim is not well established. In fact, we may eventually discover that essay questions have little distinct advantage over objective questions in measuring academic achievement (except, perhaps, in the areas of synthesis and evaluation). This is not to say that essay questions have no advantages over objective questions. It is to say that their advantages may lie elsewhere.

The most important aspect of essay questions is that they provide relative freedom of response. Whenever you want your students to select from an array of information, organize what they select, and express themselves in writing with a minimum of constraint, the essay question is unequaled. That is their main advantage. And surely the ability to write a quality essay about a subject of interest is a very important educational outcome.

But there are some serious drawbacks: First, the scoring of essays is inconsistent (unreliable). Studies have shown that teachers will independently assign a range of scores to the same essay paper. Further, any one teacher may well change his assessments of a set of essay papers from one scoring session to another. Second, because only a relatively small number of questions can be asked in a typical testing session, essay tests tap a smaller sample of student achievement than do objective tests (this also weakens reliability). And third, because the item-writer is seldom called on to reveal her scoring methods, item and scoring deficiencies are less open to scrutiny than are deficiencies in objective test items.

Guidelines for Constructing Essays

1. Use essay items to assess complex learning outcomes. Avoid starting essay questions with terms like list, name, state, who, what, where, and when. You are likely to end up with written-response items when you do. To encourage higher forms of thinking, consider using such words or phrases as compare, argue for or against, speculate about the causes for, reorganize, hypothesize, take a position and defend it, and so on.

2. Favor restricted-response essays. It is generally advisable to construct essays that can be answered in about 15 minutes. Following this guideline will provide a broader sampling of student achievement. The scorer's task also will be more manageable.

3. Structure the problem. Structure is provided when items specify what students are to do and the basis on which their answers will be judged. Additional information, such as how long students should work on an essay, is also recommended, as in the example of an extended-response essay item presented earlier.

4. Prepare model answers before asking students to respond. Following this guideline will help you decide which questions need to be altered or eliminated.

5. Allow sufficient time to answer. There is some tendency to ask too many essay questions in a single testing period. This can result in frantic efforts to write as much as possible; in the end, quality is sacrificed for quantity. If students are to think and outline before they write, they must have time to do so.

6. Encourage thoughtful answers. You might try this out:

   a) Prepare model answers (guideline 4); then
   b) give students more time to answer than you needed; and

c) let students know that thoughtful answers are expected by giving them access to earlier model answers, requesting that they think and outline before writing, and scoring all essays carefully — this includes writing positive and constructive negative comments on each essay paper.

7. Require all students to answer the same questions. Letting students decide which of several questions to answer may be the popular thing to do, but it is bad practice when instructional objectives are the same for all students. When each student answers a different set of questions, the basis for comparing their answers is weakened.

Guidelines for Scoring Essays

Inconsistency in scoring essays can be diminished by following these guidelines.

1. Use model answers. Evaluate student answers by comparing them to the model answers prepared before the test. You may need to adjust model answers slightly to accommodate student response patterns. This is the most important scoring guideline.

2. Score the same question on all papers before going on to the next question. Focusing on one question at a time across papers will help you compare answers.

3. Cover student names. If possible, keep from identifying the essay writer. Following this guideline will reduce the likelihood of biased scoring.

4. Read each essay twice before scoring. Better still, ask a colleague to spot-check your scoring. Putting this guideline into effect may be close to impossible for busy teachers. Nevertheless, reading essays more than once is likely to increase scoring accuracy.

Perhaps enough has been said about the do's and don'ts of item-writing. The next chapter provides practice in applying some of the suggestions.

Some Practice

The following items violate one or more of the guidelines presented in the last chapter. A few items may be acceptable. To provide clarity, the items are written at the knowledge or comprehension level. See if you can spot the problems with these items.

True-False Items

1. The most important aspect of essay questions is that they provide relative freedom of response.
2. Mozart's contribution to symphonic music has been extensive.
3. Criminologists sometimes disagree about the use of punishment to diminish crime.

Let's see how you have done. Item 1 fails to identify the source of the opinion. The word "extensive" in Item 2 needs to be qualified; otherwise the item will remain ambiguous. Item 3 uses a specific determiner (sometimes) and is trivial.

Completion Items

4. Another (name) for table of specifications is test blueprint.
5. If a teacher wants to evaluate skills in selecting, organizing, and synthesizing, she should favor an (essay) item.
6. The Empire State Building is in (New York).

Item 4 suffers from two problems: the blank is in the beginning rather than near the end of the question, and the answer is unimportant. It would be easy to rewrite the question so that the answer is table of specifications or test blueprint. Did you spot the grammatical giveaway in Item 5? The "an" before the blank eliminates all objective-type items considered in this fastback! Item 6 is slightly open. What should one do with "mid-Manhattan?" It can be repaired by adding mid-Manhattan to the key or adding "the city of" to the item.

Multiple-Choice Items

7. Which of the following qualify as objective test items?
   a. True-false
   b. Multiple-choice
   c. Restricted-response essay
   d. a and b
   e. b and c

8. Reliability
   a. refers to consistency in measurement
   b. is a synonym for objectivity
   c. refers to the error portion of a score
   d. declines as the length of a test increases

9. Morphemes consist of one or more
   a. clauses
   b. words
   c. phonemes
   d. sentences

Note the grammatical giveaway in Item 7 — the plural stem directs students away from options "a," "b," and "c." Thus only two viable options remain. Item 8 illustrates a very common fault — the item stem fails to present a complete problem. Finally, what do you suppose an uninformed student would do with Item 9? Undoubtedly some would receive credit by merely associating the similar-looking words, morphemes and phonemes.

Essay Items

10. Tell all you know about the Treaty of Guadalupe Hidalgo.
11. What is content validity?
12. Discuss achievement testing.

Item 10: Many years ago I responded as a fifth-grader to this exact item. I answered correctly (I said I knew nothing about the treaty), but received no credit for my sincere effort. The teacher remained impervious to my complaints. This item, as defined in this fastback, is at best a written-response question. Needless to say, I think it should be stated a little differently.

Like the previous question, Item 11 calls for knowledge or comprehension. It, too, will probably function as a written-response question.

Item 12: Volumes have been written about achievement testing. What is to be discussed? Teacher-made tests? Standardized achievement testing? Norms and their interpretation? Validity issues? Paper-and-pencil or other forms of achievement testing? If students have 20 or 60 minutes to answer, they must know what is expected and how their answers will be evaluated. Lack of structure, as in the case of this item, is likely to provoke both a wide range of answers and subjectivity in scoring.

A Closing Note

Following the PLAN-WRITE system will help you prepare good, content-valid tests. But once your tests have been administered, there is an additional step to be taken. You should do an item analysis. An item analysis provides information about item difficulty (items that are too difficult or too easy will hurt test reliability) and item discrimination (you may want to know how well items discriminate between high-achieving and low-achieving students). Acting on the results of an item analysis can improve the general quality of a test. The references on the next page will help you locate simple item analysis procedures.

Finally, let me urge you to continue your studies. Whether you are concerned with item writing, item analysis, using tests for non-grading purposes, criterion versus norm-referenced testing, standardized tests and their interpretation, or most other topics in educational evaluation, you will find the literature in the area well-developed and helpful.

Sources for Additional Information on Measurement and Evaluation

T he following two books are highly recommended. Consult the first one if you want scope and depth. It includes a chapter on item analysis for classroom tests and extended discussions on standardized testing. The Tuckman book is considerably shorter and written for the practitioner. Both touch on Benjamin Bloom's work.

Hopkins, K.D; Stanley, J.C.; and Hopkins, B.R. *Educational and Psychological Measurement and Evaluation*. 7th ed. Englewood Cliffs, N.J.: Prentice-Hall, 1990.

Tuckman, B.W. *Testing for Teachers*. 2nd ed. San Diego: Harcourt Brace Jovanovich, 1988.